She Is My Daughter:

He Is His Son

Luna Verner

Dedication

I DEDICATE THIS book to my treasured daughter, who is now using her voice, walking with truth and wholeness into her destiny. I thank you, daughter, for the extensive hours of therapy (days and nights), facing hard truths, crying, and forgiving. We started our journey figuratively on crutches, limping through life. We then forged through the fire together on the journey of healing what was once a poor communicative, crippled relationship of broken emotions, old patterns and systems of false conclusions, mental attitudes of judgment, negative words, thoughts, and actions forging ahead through the fire together into a new journey of healing.

As I look at you going through the spiritual transformation, you are blossoming into an even more beautiful woman of God. My precious daughter, walk at unlimited capacity confidently, making sharper turns and bolder moves in your God-given purpose. Stay laser-focused, listen to God's voice, and do not let any person, place, or thing distract, slow down, or stop your momentum!

Acknowledgment

Life is full of people who come and go—some make lifelong impressions, while others are just there to test your character. I would like to take this time to acknowledge two ladies who had faith in my vision to write my story as part of my healing process after leaving a 50-year marriage.

I thank you, Lisa Thomas and Patricia Miller, for supporting me financially to purchase a laptop so that I can share my story with the world. I greatly respect you for being so resolute during my healing journey. I will always have a special place in my heart for these two ladies, who are angels sent from God!

About the Author

Luna was dedicated to the constitution of marriage, vowing never to divorce. She gave her all to make it work. It was not until 50 years later, she had an epiphany identifying years of red flags. Luna took a leap of faith, left with nothing but a small suitcase, and a small monthly social security check, pursued her purpose and destiny.

Luna Verner was the fifth child of seven. She came from a structured family, where love abode. Her father owned a well-established dry cleaning business. Her mother was an outstanding seamstress, who could upholster furniture, make her own patterns out of newspaper, and create any type of garment a person could imagine. Her parents' business savvy labeled them a power couple of their era. Luna watched the dynamics of her parents' marriage, believing one day she would have love displayed to her, as her Father did for her Mother regularly. Her parents were married for 58 years, until her mother passed at 86 years old.

Table of Contents

Introduction

The line in the sand has been drawn, mother and daughter on one side of the sand, while father and son on the other side of the sand. Now it is time to face another reality of whom my out-of-sync marriage had affected, in addition to my husband and myself. It took me sixty-nine years to embrace the truth about my marriage and another two years to become aware of the humungous elephant of a problem before a resolution could be implemented. Now, I will share intricate details of what precisely the elephant is.

The first book focused on my marriage in *Book One (1), 50 Years of Marriage Blind and Bound: Deception by Manipulation,* of the Series: *Conquering the Power of Manipulation, Book Two (2)* will take you on a more profound journey, exposing how I allowed my dysfunctional marriage of fifty years to negatively affect my children from their early formative years up through adulthood. Sadly, the firstborn child has the most demanding road, which was that way for my daughter.

In this book, I share how ineffective I was when verbalizing thoughts to my daughter. I was never wrong and often dismissed her thoughts. I revealed how my controlling attitude mandated the last word, shutting down her communication with me about anything. This book conveys why parents should be open-minded and focused on making a safe place for their children to share anything with them.

Embark on this challenging journey of telling the blatant truth about a mother and father's shortcomings as parents, what I did not do with my daughter, suppressing her thoughts, and coddling my son. As a younger mother, I thought I was focused on nurturing the whole child. Instead, I touched on specific areas of their lives. Later, I realized I had fallen short and would not receive a return for what I had not poured into my daughter. What at a pompous jackass, I was the determining factor.

Book Two (2) explains why parents should spend exclusive time with their children to discuss important matters. In it, I share how I brushed off subjects that were important to my daughter and caused unnecessary hardship during her marriage and divorce. You will gain an understanding of how my old system of rapid fire from my mouth caused crippling barriers for both of my children for decades. The insight of collaborating with my daughter contributes to building a great relationship by correcting old, familiar, dysfunctional behavioral patterns.

This saga shows transparency to the readers of how I created a mama's boy by sheltering my son and the effect it had on my husband, exposing his cancerous jealousy and how it manifested. I listened to negative comments that flooded out of my husband's mouth for many years, and I will share what he covered up from childhood. Never realizing I could have redirected the course of their relationship if I had been a wiser wife and mother.

She Is My Daughter: He Is His Son expounds on how parenting is most effective when there is a united front in raising and developing healthy children, which I seldom practice at home. The most effective advice for parenting children is in the Bible: no psychologist or therapist will ever give better advice unless they direct you to instructions on child-rearing according to the Bible. I believe everything starts with how a child is raised in the home, as they tell through their actions what is happening or not happening in the house, and love is the anchor that keeps a family intact.

In my first book, I shared that family and love were prevalent; my parents did their best to teach me what they had learned about life. Once married and four years later, I displayed the love I had experienced to our children. My daughter has told me and others, "I knew and felt my parents' love." I never recall hearing my husband speak of those words with his parents.

My husband's home experience was vastly different from mine. Reflecting, I never saw my husband's parents together at their home, nor did they speak of each other in the absence of one another, as my parents would frequently do. I do not recall seeing them together at my husband's mother's last birthday party the day she passed. His dad was an absentee husband, fulfilling his adulterous appetite. If his Dad were there, his mother would be working and vice versa. Looking at our family traits, my husband and I merged a landmine of family traits into our children's lives.

The first book introduced you to generational patterns and traits. In this book, I explicitly share our family traits passed down from generation to generation, regardless of family members' awareness. I can only speculate, but somebody in my husband's family was an expert manipulator. From my experience of living with a methodical manipulator, everybody in the family feels the wrath of negative frequency. It lives in the atmosphere. With my overpowering personality and my husband's narcissism, it was no wonder there was friction and arguments all the time. Only by God's grace have our children turned out as well as they have in life!

I expound on solutions for addressing and dealing with the negative family traits and patterns that have ruled and reigned in our family lineage for too long. I will take you on my rigorous journey as we continue to learn to identify them and become more aware of the truth to tackle them with spiritual wisdom. Those traits or unwelcome familiar spirits must be called out to exposure only through the mighty power and authority of Jesus. This has uncovered welcome spiritual freedom while paving a positive path for future generations of the family and sharing resolutions of how we are conquering manipulation.

In Book One (1), *50 Years of Marriage Blind and Bound: Deception by Manipulation*, I discussed when my husband's dad abandoned him the night of his mother's funeral for his mistress of eighteen years. My husband was eighteen years old when his mother died, and the mistress was in his father's life for eighteen years before he finally married her; what does that imply? If I figured it out, did anybody in his family do the same? No teenager recovers from that without professional or spiritual guidance or wisdom from someone who has experienced similar circumstances.

My husband, who could have been living out his fantasy of what he wanted his dad to be, was a fun dad who regularly took the children to Malibu Speed Zone, Putt-Putt Golfing, West End Arcades, and Go-Carts. Raising children involves many layers, such as being prepared for challenging times and being aware of coping with circumstances. For a parent, this takes a lot of love and patience.

My husband did not know how to take our son under his wing for guidance because he had never had that experience. I only saw my husband's father engaging in him when he was being challenged to race or play basketball. Oh yes, a few times, his father assisted as a Handyman. Lord, bless his heart. I also did not take my daughter under my wing, as my mother attempted to do with her daughters. We both failed in that category; had there been a rating, we both would have received big fat F's!

As parents, how often do we forget that we lead by example, good or bad? Everyone has good and bad traits, so I will take this time to elaborate on sound characteristics. He had some positive qualities I appreciated, such as performing essentials such as house payments, keeping the yard meticulously groomed (weeds did not have a chance), paying all household bills and car insurance, having clean vehicles, and even washing clothes (he never had a problem going to the washateria, years before we could afford our washer and dryer). The house was never in disarray or not clean. My husband has Obsessive Compulsive Disorder (OCD), which often worked to our family's advantage since I worked outside of the home as well. When it came to spending money, my husband was a tightwad!

We had to have something in common that drew us to each other. We were both on the same page regarding paying bills, maintaining excellent credit, and work ethics. Those things were few but essential for our household. In those areas, we had a united front. We emphasized the importance of acquiring and maintaining excellent credit and discussed it with each child. My husband paid for our daughter's car when she was eighteen, and our son received a car in high school when he was seventeen.

Unfortunately, when it came to having a united front as parents, getting my husband to take his rightful position was a struggle, so I had to do it! Maybe seeing his dad being beyond an alpha man swayed my husband in the other direction. In our family, history repeated itself, as my husband's manipulation conditioned our daughter to suppress most of her feminine side, causing her to be abrasive, just like her mother. My overbearing actions sucked all the air out of the room, causing my daughter to be stifled in voicing her opinion. That trait showed up in our daughter at the most inconvenient time in her life, causing unnecessary complications.

At twenty-three, I thought I knew what was essential to my daughter; I had to mimic what I saw my mother doing with her five girls, right? Years later, I realized no generic method existed, but it should be customized to the child. As my daughter matured, her thoughts and actions differed from mine. She was more astutely aware of specific things than I was at her age. She wanted to articulate and think for herself; she expressed that it was a new era, not the 1960s, and she was right!

I was a novice at raising a free-thinking daughter and a novice at raising my son, so I concentrated on what I knew: how to instill a religious foundation. Looking back, I should have taught the children how to have a relationship with God, not religion, which I will discuss later. I was so unfair by assuming things with my daughter because I was a female, yet I did research for books on male puberty. Desiring to become a better parent, I purchased books on parenting, but I wanted my husband to be included. Waiting for him to engage, the books accumulated dust. Frustrated and disappointed, I gave them to a young couple at church who had just had a baby.

I got my mind blown when I went to the library to find books on puberty in male children and discovered they have five stages. I was determined to mold my son into the type of husband I wanted his dad to be, but that was a revelation later in life. My son and I would study bible lessons together and then discuss them. I thought I was protecting my son from my husband by coddling him and being my son's mouthpiece, but I caused resentment from my husband and daughter for decades and later from my son.

This book will clarify why I state, "She Is My Daughter: He Is His Son." This saga tells the effects of how my children coped with dysfunctional parents living a lie of a marriage in a household and how it showed up in my children's lives and marriages.

The aftermath was tumultuous, and there is a negative residual in my son's life that surfaces in the form of bitterness against me, especially once I left my husband. His hostile words were often out of order. From a mother's perspective, he temporarily lost his spiritual mind, forgetting his position, forever a son in the family. He was not practicing what he was preaching. I am confident that God will direct him back to grace, away from legalism, and onto the correct path once he allows his heart to accept the truth. I am keeping the faith that the gentle giant suppressed deep inside of my son will surface as a mature, spiritual giant, walking in the truth and fullness of God.

My daughter is more conscious of what has transpired for so many years, and her gradual spiritual maturity is a significant factor in her coping through her life now. She understands that family patterns have and will become broken for future generations. She and I have come together to consistently work to break those patterns and be free in Jesus!

Both children are on pilgrim journeys by God's power, grace, and mercy. Our daughter participates in multiple women's ministries, spreading the gospel of Jesus Christ's eternal salvation while walking out God's word daily! Our son, God help him, is a head-strong, out-of-the-box thinking minister marching offbeat to his drum. He and his wife are raising their children to be spirit-led solid rocks for Jesus! The fruit is bearing itself, as the oldest grandson, at the time of this book, ten years old, has been on social media, encouraging people to never give up in life!

My son and daughter-in-law, married fifteen years, during the time of this book, observed the flaws of my marriage, and did the opposite, in their marriage. They are passionately educating other married couples on how to sustain a healthy, solid marriage. The faults in my marriage, contributed to the my son's marriage thriving, as he and his wife implement strong communication skills, and putting God in the forefront of their marriage.

Shots Fired!

MY HUSBAND RAN out of our bedroom with his snub-nose shotgun and aimed it at our daughter. He threatened to use it on her; the mama bear in me rushed to intervene; like a tsunami, I fearlessly stepped into the altercation. My husband could have quickly shot me, but there was no way on earth I was going to let my only daughter become harmed by my intoxicated husband. I was not afraid to face the barrel of the shotgun. My daughter had no clue that listening to threatening words while having a gun pointed in my face was nothing new to me. I had been in that precarious position multiple times. I gazed down the barrel of my husband's nine-millimeter handgun at least four times after he and I moved to the country. I had no fear of dying, for I knew if he ever pulled the trigger, I would be at peace with God! Let me share how I go from celebrating my sixty-ninth birthday to almost meeting Jesus!

My caring, thoughtful daughter relocated back to Texas in September 2022. Now that she lived back home with us, she wanted to do something special for my birthday. We started celebrating my birthday at an upscale nail salon and planned to conclude the evening with a nice dinner. The nail salon offered complimentary alcoholic beverages. I knew I would want a birthday drink later in the evening, so I only had one cocktail. My daughter also only had one drink, knowing we would partake in a birthday celebration drink later. That was not the case with my husband, who did not know when to stop drinking. The nail salon manager was particularly fond of us, so every time my husband finished one drink, the salon manager quickly refilled his glass, which led to the beginning of his anger from embarrassment.

This was one of the top ten embarrassing moments of my life. I knew my husband had a high tolerance for liquor, but he went beyond his drinking ability this time. Unbelievably, I had never seen him in this stage of inebriation in public. He was on his fourth strong drink and thought he was fine; however, when he tried to get out of the pedicure chair to sit on the salon working stool, he slid out of the chair, and his shoes flew off his feet, going two different directions, as his glass shattered spilling liquor over the floor. His fall scared everyone in the salon, especially me. In the fifty years of marriage, I had never seen him so inebriated. The sad part about the incident is that he kept asking for another drink. Once my husband pulled himself up from the floor, he tried to sit in one of the chairs with wheels. He missed the chair and burst his butt on the floor, looking as if someone had pulled the chair from under him. One time, falling could have been a misstep, but falling out of a chair twice was a sure sign that my husband had gone overboard with drinking. My daughter suggested that her dad rest in the car until the nail technician finishes working on our nails.

Concerned about the liability for injuries, the manager told my husband that there would be no more drinks for him. The technician working on my nails got so nervous that he started filing my nails like he was filing prison bars. My hand got extremely hot, and I yelled, "Hey, you are hurting my hand!" He explained that his dad had an alcoholic addiction and watched my husband give him flashbacks of what his family endured. My husband had taken the technician back to a horrible experience of his father's reckless drinking and how it affected his whole family. The technician was over fifty years old and still bears the scars of his dad's addiction. I asked the technician to calm down and take a deep breath before continuing to work on my nails.

Complaining with every step, my husband went to the car to sleep off his inebriation, or so I thought, but he was on the telephone talking to his best friend, the third wheel in my marriage. After completing my nails, I apologized to the staff and tipped them generously for their services. My daughter suggested that her Dad needed food in his system. She thought my husband had calmed down from the falls. That was not the case; my husband waited for us to get into the car to give me a piece of his mind as if I had caused his falls.

From the moment my daughter began driving to the restaurant until we arrived at our destination, my husband expressed his dissatisfaction with me, using foul, distasteful words. Fortunately, I was in my new, improved, positive Christ-like mindset, not responding to his belligerent behavior, so I stayed quiet. Once arriving at the restaurant, my daughter and I had a birthday celebration drink. My husband also ordered a drink, putting more fuel on his fire as he got on his bandwagon about how irritated I had made him.

Sitting in the restaurant, my husband complained about me getting my nails done. He yelled, "We had no problems until our daughter moved back home and encouraged you to start wasting money." Guess who paid for my upgraded look — me! He did not contribute one penny to my nails, clothes, or hair.

My daughter told me one day, weeks before my birthday celebration, "Mom, just because you live in the country does not mean you have to look like it." That day, I immediately went to my bathroom and looked in the mirror at myself; my thick salt-colored twisted hair, resembling Ceely from The Color Purple, and my clothes shouted Raggedy Ann. I emphatically agreed with my daughter's statement! I looked pathetic and had utterly lost my identity! Taking a stand, I ordered seven outfits with sandals to match. My daughter told my husband that most men want to see their spouses or partners look attractive. I dressed differently when I worked and lived in the city, but it went downhill when we moved to the country.

My husband became more insecure once I stepped up my game to look better and discarded the long dresses, jean skirts with T-shirts, and leggings underneath, which I call Raggedy Ann clothes. My husband thought I might attract other men, as he always told me I deserved better. However, he never tried to become better, but I was committed to my marriage and did not believe in divorce, which I am now aware was prideful idolatry.

I had made my marriage an idol for years. I would often boast about how long my marriage had lasted, but what does it matter the years if it is not a Godly ordained covenant marriage? Longevity means nothing if your children become altered by their parents' ignorance of how to pour into their true personalities. I am so thankful for the grace and mercy God bestowed upon us as parents who walked in cluelessness instead of leading our children to the light of Christ's instructions.

The conversation escalated, and my husband raised his voice in the restaurant and again cussed at me. It did not matter what terrible words my husband said to me; I was not going to argue. My daughter was seeing something new in her mother. She realized there was a transformation unfolding from my old patterns. From the formative years of my daughter's life up until now, I was the parent who would tear my husband to shreds with harsh, hurtful words, and I would have the last say, but now I was silent*

My daughter, for the first time in her life, saw who the original hell raiser was; she asked my husband to stop dishonoring me and wait until we got home to finish his ranting. Our daughter told her Dad that she would speak up for him if I were cussing and dishonoring him, so she was speaking to her mother's defense. We finished our dinner, and as soon as we got back into my daughter's car, nasty spirits of rage and hostility showed themselves front and center. My husband started cussing at my daughter, but she was ready for the battle.

Remember, my husband had groomed this daughter to care for herself physically. As my daughter was driving, my husband was trying to hit her while she was at a disadvantage. I put my hand on the top of my daughter's car seat to block contact from my husband's swinging, so I took the hits. My husband provoked my daughter into a yelling rage as she drove extremely fast on the busy expressway. At one point, I was afraid we would end up in a crash as my daughter weaved in and out of the lanes, going well over the speed limit of seventy-five miles per hour.

Travel time home, under normal conditions, would take one and one-half hours, but this time, it only took forty-five minutes. The yelling got worse, and by the time we finally reached home, both parties were ready to throw blows. The arguing continued from the driveway into the house. Her dad was spewing out profanity at the top of his voice. My husband fed off negativity, so he continued ranting throughout the home. When he came out of the bedroom, he did not have the usual nine-millimeter handgun that he had pulled on me multiple times. Instead, he had his snub-nose shotgun. My daughter was standing by a loveseat responding to her dad's outburst, and before I realized it, my husband was walking towards my daughter with his shotgun. I stepped between them, facing my husband with solid feet on the floor, bracing myself for whatever came next. Startled and shocked by my actions, my husband realized I would take a bullet and die before letting him harm our daughter. My fearless attitude startled my husband. I could see it in his eyes, which brought him back to his senses from what he was about to do. He turned around and took the shotgun back to the bedroom. I was so disgusted with my husband's actions. What a fool I was to put up with that type of treatment for the final five years of marriage. Now, my daughter has seen the horrible version of her dad. She had never seen this raging maniac! This was not the fun, playful, loving dad she had always adored.

My husband and daughter went to bed angry, not to mention how hurt I was by everything that had transpired. My husband was so out of it that he did not remove his clothes; he fell asleep on the bed. As I lay in the bed, I was uneasy and restless. I felt my spirit battling against evil spirits within my husband. A heavy, combative spiritual battle of good and evil was going on between us. This was a strange feeling I had never experienced in our marriage. I lay in bed for twenty minutes praying, unable to get a peaceful breakthrough for rest. Following my better judgment, I went to sleep on the couch. That was the first time I had slept outside my bedroom in fifty years of marriage. I am sure it was in my best interest. Who knows what my husband might have done to me?

My husband was comfortable pointing a gun at me and getting up the following day as if nothing had happened. With my low self-worth, I had conditioned his toxic behavior to be just another day, no big deal. That incident of my husband pointing a shotgun at our daughter should have been a top priority for discussion the following day, but it never happened. Once my husband, daughter, and I had slept from that horrible incident, I thought the next day we would all sit down and recap what happened and why, with apologies to follow. That is not what happened. When I asked my husband when a suitable time would be to discuss what happened last night, he replied, "I do not want to talk about what happened, now or anytime; just forget about it."

The whole week, my husband functioned as if that horrible incident never happened. Was he that disconnected, or did he not care? I realized that I was to blame for that attitude; I had conditioned my husband to believe there were no consequences for his poor behavior when he had pointed his gun at me so many times. At that time, there were no boundaries or accountability for unacceptable actions. My husband conducted himself inappropriately by pulling a gun on me, so it was no problem to pull a gun on his daughter.

My daughter is my perfect likeness, so he treated her like he had been treating me. The tension in our home was so thick you could cut it with a knife. My daughter could not believe that her father would treat her the way he did, and she stayed over at a friend's house for a few days. This was the result of my husband doing what I had allowed him to do — pointing a gun at your wife without consequences or repercussions. I never called the police department, but I should have, and there would have been a paper trail. That would have shown my husband that you cannot point a gun at people and get away with it. Now, my husband has pulled a gun on every member of our family - myself, my daughter, and my son.

Yes, you heard what I just admitted: there had been an incident where my husband pointed his gun at our son. The relationship between my son and husband would go south whenever my husband questioned our son's disciplinary actions towards our oldest grandson. At that time, he was a nervous little boy because my son yelled at him regularly. This was not the understanding son that had been the voice of reason. My son changed his mannerisms after marriage, just as I had done in my marriage. However, his wife did not change our son's mannerisms; what did will be discussed later.

Both my husband and son have quick tempers and can go from zero to one hundred in a matter of seconds. I once had a terrible temper, but I decided to change my way after my daughter was born. I toned it down so my daughter would not see the rage that my husband had activated in me, and our son never saw that side of me. That is a perfect example of how familiar patterns surface within the family. Even though my son had never seen my raging fits of anger, it lay dormant inside of him until the perfect situation activated and brought it to the surface.

My husband and I made a terrible decision that quickly went awry. We sold the family home in the city, built a custom-manufactured home, and quickly moved onto our son's land. This was one of the top ten most significant mistakes we could have made besides marrying each other. No matter how old your children become, there should always be a level of respect towards their parents. That was not the case with our son, who lived according to what he had seen. Our son began treating us like children, forgetting the family hierarchy.

The residual of the incident bled over to using the grandchildren as pawns of leverage, as he did so often. He allowed us to have the grandsons over when it benefited our son, which equated to about three weeks later. We had to go to our son's home, thirty feet from our home, to visit our grandsons, which broke my heart. I often planned creative activities for my grandsons when they visited our house, and I always cooked unique dishes they had not eaten before. I had waited years to become a grandmother, and now my son had stripped it away.

As mentioned, our son did not like my husband's comment on how he chastised our grandson, nor did I approve. This time, I watched the two most important men I love yell across the driveway at each other. When my son and husband had their heated disagreement, my husband pulled out his nine-millimeter gun on our son, waving it in the air.

This was not the first time my husband had provoked our son, but it was the most damaging. Our son ran into his house and came back with his rifle. My son walked up and down his side of the driveway while his dad stood on our steps, yelling as if they were two strangers. I could not believe what I saw and how irrational and crazy they acted. I continued to speak to my husband and son a second time, asking them to put their guns away and talk through the situation or go inside their homes. Both men were so angry they heard nothing that I said.

Living in the country, having a handgun strapped in its holster was not unusual because we never knew what wild animal we might have encountered on the land. While working outside, I wore my husband's second nine-millimeter in a holster strapped to my thigh, around my leggings. I used it three times to kill snakes and animals. This was going to be the fourth occurrence to use my gun. The difference between my husband, son, and myself was that I never pulled my gun from its holster unless I was going to use it.

I continued to listen as the conversation got louder and louder as the two family members argued. I tried to reason with them, but my words landed on deaf ears. I thought if they did not listen to my words, I would go into the back of the property and let them hear shots fired in hopes that they would wonder what had happened and why I, of all people, was firing my gun. After firing my weapon four times, I returned to the scene of confusion between my husband and son. They stopped arguing after hearing four shots were fired and finally came to their senses, realizing how deadly their actions could have been. Thank God for wisdom. My out-of-the-box thinking avoided what could have been a double tragedy.

The two incidents were significantly different, with our children having their dad pull a gun on them both. My husband was far more aggressive with our daughter than he had ever been with our son. It would have been different if our son's and husband's sizes were compatible. Instead, our son stands over six feet tall and weighs over three hundred pounds. Where our daughter is five feet two inches and one hundred fifty pounds, could my husband have been more aggressive with our daughter than our son because she perfectly resembles me, and our son resembles his father? Or was he showing whom he had become, a man holding extreme resentment in his heart for his family?

Image in the Mirror

IT IS INCREDIBLE how strong DNA traits children can pull back through generations we never met. When our children look at their images in the mirror, there is an uncanny younger version of their parents. My daughter and I look so much alike that people have told her she looks like my clone. My daughter looks exactly like me, and aspects of our lives have been parallel.

My daughter entered the world quickly. I only had to endure under eight hours of labor, which made her birth extremely easy for me. She was born at the hospital where her dad worked, so his coworkers were amazed to see his bundle of joy appear so fair-skinned that they assumed she was Caucasian. To me, our daughter looked more like a bright-skinned Native American baby. My husband's coworkers jokingly told him he had better find the real daddy because it could not have been him. In my first book, I broke down the diverse cultures in my bloodline. My daughter's great-grandmothers' (my father's and mother's moms) DNA dominated.

My daughter has always been strong-willed and intelligent. She was potty trained and walking at nine months old. I knew then that I had to stay one step ahead of her, ensuring she did not get bored with learning. When she was three years old, I wrote words for everything in her bedroom to jump-start her process of learning how to read. She was like a human sponge, soaking up every word introduced to her, realizing reading was the key to learning about the world. I would read to her every day. She would see me reading my Reader's Digest, so she would grab her books and read them at the age of four.

I did not realize how much of myself I had poured into my daughter until she started preschool, which showed in her studies. When I bought a collection of Black historical books, our daughter read every one without prompting. Unfortunately, I was also pouring my dysfunctional, contagious behavior into her personality. I taught her poor communication skills, how to be a smart mouth, and how to cuss, in addition to other poor qualities that I have regretted.

Where was my husband? He was flipping out, trying to grasp the full-time responsibilities of supporting a family, which was why I returned to work. My husband would not have had any children had I not wanted them. He was more a babysitter than a dad, being a fun parent, so what child would not gravitate to a parent who had never disciplined or seldom scolded a child for anything? My husband, the expert manipulator, would tell me what our daughter had done wrong so I could be the disciplinarian, keeping him in our daughter's good grace and labeling me as the mean parent!

My husband's family was overflowing with male grandsons. Our daughter was not the first granddaughter, but the first granddaughter my husband's family could enjoy from birth until we moved from Oklahoma to Texas. Surprisingly, my husband's oldest brother had two beautiful older daughters whom we met years after our daughter was born. His brother's third daughter is the same age as our daughter. They all reside in Tulsa, Oklahoma.

Parenthood did not agree with my husband as it did with me. As the years passed, he taught our daughter an appreciation of music, which flowed through my husband's veins, taking her to the record store to listen to old-school records. He also taught her practical skills, such as driving a stick-shift car, changing a tire, and paying bills. On the other hand, I instructed our daughter never to be afraid to work for what you want out of life or give up on your goals.

Dad was always the fun guy who seldom disciplined our daughter. I do not recall one time my husband disciplined our daughter for anything. My husband did all the fun stuff with our daughter, such as go-carts, bike riding, skating, playing arcade and video games, doing his dance called the crank, and fighting.

In Book One (1), "50 Years of Marriage Blind and Bound: Deception by Manipulation," of the Series: Conquering the Power of Manipulation, I explained why I returned to work. It was time for our precious little girl to experience socializing with children her age, so we needed to place her in an environment that would prepare her for public school.

Little did I realize in the seventies that I was home-schooling our daughter, letting my creative ideas flow long before completing my Interdisciplinary Studies degree. I was the teacher and disciplinarian with my daughter. Our daughter could talk with any adult, and most times, they would ask her, "Are you sure you are only four years old?" My husband and I knew this head-strong little girl needed a school with structure, so we decided she would attend a private preschool!

My husband and I wanted the best for our daughter, so we enrolled her in Montessori preschool minutes away from her Dad's job after weeks of looking for the right preschool to enhance her eagerness to learn. She was always so inquisitive, just like me when I was young, but unlike me, she would not rest until she had her questions answered.

We grew up in a Baptist religious denomination; she had no exposure to any other religions when she was four years old. At six years old, my daughter and I broke free from the Baptist religion and discovered the joy of Pentecostal worship. We both enjoyed the upbeat music, multiple instruments, tambourines, dancing, and seeing God's Holy Spirit move upon the people.

This was the first time our daughter attended a Catholic preschool, and she wanted to know what was under the nun's coifs, so she pulled off the head nun's coif to see if she was bald or had hair. Once my daughter had reached an answer to her question, she moved on to her next adventure of discovery. The nuns used the disciplinary ruler to chastise the preschoolers, but that did not intimidate our daughter. That did not stop our little girl from doing whatever came to her mind.

My daughter expressed through her actions how she felt not being home with her mom and getting the full attention she was accustomed to receiving. One problem when working the day shifts I never got off work early enough to pick up our daughter, and my husband had to be the receiver of the disruptions our daughter caused at school regularly. Now that I think back on the situation, it served him right; he needed to hear the nuns complain about fighting her classmates since he was the one who made our daughter tougher than beef jerky! Neither I nor my husband was aware that he was preparing her for later in life.

Here is a prime example of how tough my husband had groomed our daughter to become. One Sunday, I had completed alterations for my husband, and my sewing machine was on top of the dresser. I did not have a stand to encase the sewing machine when using it, so that location was my sewing station. I had instructed our daughter not to touch the machine because it was unstable.

That meant nothing to our four-year-old daughter, so what happened was that the sewing machine fell and broke her leg. The sewing machine hit her leg and bounced off because when I ran into the room, the machine was in one location, and she was in another. She told us her leg was hurting; we saw her limping but had no clue she had broken her right leg. She did not cry; our tough little girl walked on a broken leg for the remainder of that day.

Monday, her dad took her to his job to get X-rays; the bones looked as if someone had taken a knife, making a smooth, clean cut through both bones. My husband and I thought maneuvering with a cast on her leg would be awkward for our daughter. Our daughter used her cast as a weapon with the children in preschool. I had never seen such a small cast do so much damage; I had never seen anybody use a cast for a lethal weapon. Our daughter would walk faster with the cast than she had in the past without it. Thank God, there was no permanent damage from having a broken leg!

Previously, I told you that my daughter was brilliant. After she graduated from preschool, the world was hers for the taking. When she entered kindergarten, she was reading at a second-grade level. My daughter excelled in elementary school in all subjects. Our daughter challenged her teachers to go the extra mile in teaching, as she and a few other classmates needed advanced assignments to keep their interest. I will never forget her sixth-grade graduation service.

During the seventies, Oklahoma elementary schools included the sixth grade. Our daughter delivered the sixth-grade class speech and had two days to learn a two-page speech; she nailed it. She ranked second brightest student in her grade and landed the title of Salutatorian.

The Valedictorian was a sharp, intelligent young boy who became her best friend. His mother was a genius, and I am confident this young man works in a prominent position overseas. This young boy could speak three languages back then, as his mother prepared him for life to the fullest. My daughter lost contact with her best friend when we moved to Texas.

History repeats itself; our duplex in Texas was a few houses from my middle brother-in-law's house. In my first book, I shared how my father lived next door to his two brothers; I was in a comparable situation. It was a blessing and a curse because whenever my husband's brother needed money or transportation, he would call.

Unfortunately, this brother-in-law was a pushover, and his second wife took full advantage of his weakness. The manipulating familiar spirit skipped this middle brother but landed on the oldest and youngest sons. Every wife he had ran the show, and he followed their lead. Quite frankly, my husband's male siblings were weak-minded womanizers, a familiar spirit passed down generations from decades ago. My husband's father and grandfather were Alpha males. Maybe that familiar spirit came from his mother's side of the family.

Suppose you have never heard the term familiar spirits. They are good and evil familiar traits established long before we were born that follow each generation and are known as generational curses or generational blessings. Some evil familiar spirits are dormant, just waiting for a traumatic event to happen so they can rise inside of a person. We all have them; after the evil familiar spirits are exposed and one is ready to be confronted by the truth, the challenging spiritual work begins with getting and staying free, also known as deliverance. This means one is spiritually free from the evil familiar spirits that fight tooth and nail to keep their position of negatively directing a person. These familiar spirits move with a person, no matter where one might live.

Moving to a new state is usually more challenging for the children as they adjust, losing friends and familiarity. We lived down the street from our daughter's elementary school, so she was excited to ride her new red bike instead of Mom or Dad driving her to school. When school was over, she came out excited to get home to share her first day of school. When she went to get her bike, it was gone. Somebody got a great bike at my daughter's expense; someone in the neighborhood stole it — welcome to Texas! That incident alerted our family, letting us know we were now in an environment that stretched our awareness of people from a new point of view! That was a revelation for our family. It made us more aware of our surroundings.

The old saying, "An idol mind is the devil's workshop," is true! I wanted to ensure our daughter occupied her mind on positive things, as I had as a girl. We had not found a church, so having her involved in religious activities was impossible, so I looked for other avenues. I was adamant about finding something to keep her occupied after school. A neighbor informed us about a swimming team tryout in our new town of Richardson, Texas. I thought that would be perfect for our daughter since she was like a fish in the water.

Our daughter, at the age of four, was trained to swim by a professional swimming instructor, fearless in the water and well-prepared to swim. Also, our daughter's godfather, now a medical doctor in Edmond, Oklahoma, was a licensed swimming guard who contributed to her swimming skills. We attended the tryouts and watched her confidently perform several strokes as requested without hesitation.

The swimming coach was impressed with our daughter's strong swimming skills when sharing the news that our daughter had aced the tryouts. She was the only African American little girl who tried out for the team. Our daughter often mentioned wanting to be the first African American girl to swim in the Olympics. She swam like she was born and raised in the water. There was only one barrier: a required signup fee of $175.00 to join the team. I asked if there were scholarships for candidates who could not provide the cost, but none were available. Instead of her Dad trying to figure out how to gather the funds, he told our daughter she would not be on the team. She was not happy, and neither was I.

That was an opportunity for her dad to go the extra mile and figure out how to get that money to make his daughter's dream come true. We will never know how far our daughter could have gone with her swimming abilities. However, if my husband would not go the extra mile for me, why would I expect anything different for our daughter? Looking at her reflects me; she was and still is my spitting image. Sadly, I cannot recall one time in my husband's life when he sacrificed to do more than provide customary essentials other than equating to a fun babysitter.

I had no problem sacrificing for my children, no matter what, but that is what a good mother will do for their children. I hated that I could not financially support our daughter and pay the signup fee since I had not secured work in Texas. My husband pleaded with me to stay home and not get a job, which lasted six months. To this very day, our daughter loves to swim every opportunity she gets, especially in the ocean.

When our daughter attended middle school, her grades were stellar, but life became difficult for our daughter; now, she had to deal with mean, jealous girls. Our daughter had fair skin, sandy curly hair, and a petite shape to admire, so naturally, being the new girl and grabbing several boys' attention, they wanted to see if she was a pushover. Little did the other girls know she knew how to fight, thanks to her dad. Even though she went through a short period of being bullied, she stood up for herself in the end before moving to another city.

Thank goodness my daughter and son did not pick up their dad's crazy fighting method* I saw my husband's fighting wounds from his fighting style, which was a reckoning force. I have never seen anything like that in my life. My disturbed husband would punch a person with his right hand and bite his left hand; to this day, he has permanent teeth marks between his thumb and pointer finger. I could not make a story like this if somebody offered to pay me. The closest I saw to my husband's crazy habit was my Dad biting his lip when he got upset, but that did not leave any permanent marks. As fate had it, the season was up for living in Richardson, TX. A new horizon was ahead. My husband decided he wanted to purchase a home.

I had my heart set on living in our current city, but God had different plans for our family. Interestingly, he moved on my husband to relocate our family from Richardson at an opportune time. Plano, TX, here we come!

Walking In Deception

IN 1990, WE purchased a home in Plano, Texas, and our daughter is now in ninth grade. Her school only had ninth and tenth graders, and that is when she met her first love. Like me, she had kissed a few boys, but that was as far as it went; her cookie stayed protected. Like me, she wanted a boyfriend that would lead to marriage. She had listened to the fluffy stories of how Dad and I got together; she wanted to follow in her mom's footsteps and give her cookie to only one guy, the one she would marry. Of course, she knew nothing about all the times I tried to break up with her dad and how he would threaten to kill himself. I did not want blood on my hands or to be the reason he took his life. That was a massive story of deception that should not have been told. Instead, I should have given our daughter the cold, hard facts of all the arguments her dad and I had weekly while dating.

Our daughter was a petite, cute young lady who attracted quite a few guys' interests, just as I had at that age. There was one guy who appeared to have had it all together. And just as my husband pursued me, this young man was in hot pursuit of our daughter's cookie. His parents were well-known in the community. Word on the street was that his parents burned down their house, split the insurance money, and then divorced.

His mother met a wealthy businessman who knew people in high places. This young man's mother and stepdad attended Bill Clinton's Inauguration Ball, which sealed the deal for me; this was the guy my daughter deserved. Unlike my mother, who had wisdom about my husband but did not share her thoughts with me, this guy quickly won my daughter's heart and mine. He was charismatic and privileged, and he appeared to be everything a mother would want for their daughter, which was more deception and a lie from the pits of hell! Things were in check for the first two years of our daughter's relationship with this rich boy.

Little did I know, just like my husband talked me into trusting him and becoming intimate before marriage, so did this guy convince our daughter to go for the gusto! As my daughter brought to my attention many years later, saying, "Mom, you must remember, I have half of dad's and your DNA, so my actions could reflect one or the other." This child was the one who was going to have her way, no matter the consequences.

I had always told my daughter when she thought she was ready to become intimate with a boy to let me know. That is the same thing my mother had told me. Bless her soul, she did just that, and I honestly, to this day, do not remember that happening; she told me I cussed her out and told her she was not ready for sex. In reflecting, our daughter was trying to express her feel- ings, as she should have been able to speak freely to her parents, especially her mother. I know that is when I completely stripped and robbed my daughter of having a voice with me, damaging our relationship for years to come.

I had passed down my experiences to my daughter. I was not mature when I started having sex, so I put her in the same category. She did like her mother and did precisely what I did with her dad. I am so thankful that she did not marry her high school sweetheart, who turned out to be a womanizer and a man she would always have the option to sleep with if she chose to do so, which she did not.

There has always been a different type of relationship between my two children. My daughter says she got the best version of her parents in her first seven years, even though I was controlling and intimidating. Seven years later, my son got an improved version of Mom and a not-so-good version of Dad. Our two children are seven years apart and from two different worlds.

While our daughter adjusted to the new state of Texas, our four-year-old son conquered our new neighborhood. Before moving into our house in another city, this was our first time living in a duplex; we needed a two-car garage, which would have been the perfect rental. Our duplex was across the street from a small apartment complex that housed mostly Latinos. This was our first exposure to Latin culture; we quickly became accustomed to expecting weekend parties with live music, dancing, and the aroma of great food.

Our son is the taller, super-sized, younger version of his dad, and his birth was a representation of how tough the latter years of my marriage were going to be for me. My son's birth was a sign of the hardship that was to come much later in my life. I endured sixteen hours of hard labor; I was not able to find any relief before or when I arrived at the hospital. Yes, this was the same hospital where I gave birth to my daughter. Unlike my first proud pregnancy, I was very conscious of my demeanor, what I ate, and my weight as I had vowed not to gain over thirty pounds, and I achieved that goal. I also had been so tired of fighting for my marriage that this was the year I felt defeated. Two children were born to the same parents and into the same household, one out of a mother's pride and the other out of a father's manipulation, and I love them both with all my heart.

I was eleven years into marriage, and during this pregnancy, my husband manipulated me to keep me. I ended an emotional affair a month prior with a very desirable man, who is now deceased. For inquiring readers who might wonder if my son was my emotional lover's child, no, he is not. We never met up nor had any sexual encounters, only emotional, intellectual, mind-stimulating, mature conversations over the telephone. That was one thing I admired about my emotional lover and the one thing I never received from my husband. There was no talk about sex or what he wanted to do to me, only respectful conversations about how we could unite our families and make our relation- ship work. My husband and I should have discussed those subjects regularly, but they never occurred.

I had consciously decided to have a cheerful outlook. I was determined during my third pregnancy to keep myself together and calm. I refused to give birth to a child who was fearful and lacked confidence in himself in life. I can recall one time my husband and daughter were at the dinner table eating, and I was serving dinner. Once again, my husband, who knew how to push my irritable button, said something spitefully dishonoring, referencing one of his female coworkers.

At that time in our marriage, I was working nights, and he would take my daughter to see horses at the home of a female coworker. I know he was doing it to pay me back for my emotional affair. My husband would say that this female coworker resembled me, which she did. Was there an underlying sexual desire for her in his lustful, perverted mind? His statement made me so angry that I threw a pot that shattered the dining room window, and glass shattered right next to my daughter; thank goodness she did not have one cut or scratch on her body. The old saying is true: "God takes care of fools and babies." I was the fool during that season, and my daughter was the baby.

I had my faults as a wife, but I never used The opposite sex to get under my husband's skin or irritate him into a rage. Never in my marriage did I com- pare my husband to our male friends, so I could not understand why my hus- band ridiculed me in such a way. I wanted to beat his jackass behind, but I did not fight men physically, only verbally, where I dominated every time! I could have easily accomplished that task by mentioning my ex-emotional lover, who wanted to marry me. He also worked the night shift in a different department at the same company. That was the first and last time I allowed my anger to spiral out of control to that degree.

During the pregnancy of our son, I was a different person. I was now more mature, and I had learned that the expecting mother's attitude affects the child. I had decided to be a quiet soul, but that was only during the pregnancy. In retrospect, that pregnancy took me back, for its duration, to the peaceful soul I was as a teenager before I encountered my husband!

Pregnancy is indeed the closest experience to death. When it was time for our son to arrive in the world, he came hard, weighing ten pounds, with shoul- ders broader than I could stretch, tearing me from my vagina to my rectum. He looked like he was two months old. I was watching as the doctor stuffed my insides with gauze; I did not think the bleeding would ever stop. Looking at my raw white flesh from where my son had torn me apart, I had no fear at the time. I was amazed to see my white flesh insides; I trusted God would direct my doctor to take care of the problem as I watched in the round mirror placed on the wall for mothers to see their births.

My husband stood behind the doctor with his hands crossed, and I will never forget him asking the doctor if he could repair the damage caused by our ten-pound son. I lost so much blood that the doctor wanted to do a blood transfusion. I was not in favor of that, as it was right around the time the dis- ease HIV/AIDS was rising, and there had not been a structured procedure to check donated blood for the disease. The doctor opted to put me on iron pills if I promised to take three every day for three months, and I agreed.

I had breastfed our daughter, so naturally, I wanted to do the same for our son. Feeding the baby was much easier, especially when it was late at night or early morning. My daughter was easy to breastfeed but only weighed six pounds and fourteen ounces. I had no idea what the appetite of a ten-pound baby would be until I gave birth to my son. When I breastfed him, my toes curled in from the strong suction of him feeding on my breast. Due to his enormous appetite, I had to feed him double my daughter's schedule. I had no problem producing milk, but he overate. I decided to put him on cereal when he was two months old.

Remember, I told you he looked like he was two months old at birth. He looked like he was four months old at two months old. He grew off his medical chart at one year old, and we knew then that I would need to work to feed this boy. I came from a family where the food was always plentiful, and that would not stop now that we had two children. Thank you, Jesus! To this day, we have never missed a meal, and the freezer and pantry are abundant.

I will say that staying quiet during our son's pregnancy impacted his personality. For the first three years of our son's life, he would wake up every morning with a big smile; I kid you not, that happened. God blessed me with this child being so calm. I had planned to leave my husband and start a new life with my emotional lover. My manipulative husband got me pregnant so I would not leave him for the other man, who wanted desperately to marry me. My husband was right; after getting pregnant, I would not leave the marriage or get another abortion! My children brought out the softer side of my hus- band until our son turned six years old and began playing sports. Something shifted, and my husband started emotional and verbal abuse towards our son when he started elementary school.

Our son is the total opposite of his sister but resilient. I remember he had seen Superman on television, and he wanted to fly, so he jumped off the couch, hit the coffee table, and tore his ear. Thank goodness his dad worked at a medical clinic, so he called one of the doctors to meet him to stitch our son's ear without numbing his ear. Our brave little man did not cry when the doctor stitched his ear; the doctor was impressed by his courage!

Our son inherited his Dad's family's love for music. He watched his dad create drumbeats and wanted to do the same thing. My husband would tap tunes on the dinner table, and our son would mimic the beat at a noticeably early age of three. In the 80s, rap videos were on BET regularly, and many rappers had created 800 numbers claiming one could talk to them. When his dad received the monthly telephone bill, it was $800.00; our three-year-old son had been calling the 800 number and speaking to whoever was on the other telephone line. There were no cell phones, only landlines, but we had portable phones, so he was in his bedroom dialing away. With the favor of God upon us, the phone company waived the charges once we explained what our son had done.

Our son was an animated child. He took every word to heart and was happy when his tummy was full. His dad always said that if a person offered our son food, he could have been an easy target to kidnap. He had no problems making acquaintances with children and adults. We had a block party, and our son knew people my husband and I had never met. They knew him from playing with the children in the neighborhood.

When our son was four, he looked like six and stood at my waist. We were at the grocery store, and I told him I would leave if he had not returned in time for me to finish the checkout line with the groceries. He asked me if he could get water from the fountain; I told him it was okay but to return to my line. I looked up and realized that all ten checkout lines were open, and the store was filled with people. When my son looked for me, he thought I had left him. I do not know which of us lost the other, but we could not find each other. I looked through each checkout line, but no son. I went outside the store, thinking he had gone to the next-door bakery, but there was no son! I looked for him for about thirty minutes, terrified to call my husband and tell him I had lost our son.

When I finally called my husband, he frantically asked where I was because our son was home. My husband thought someone had kidnapped me, and our son got away. This is the supernatural part of the story. We lived precisely eleven blocks from the store; it was dark. Our son told us that an angel carried him home; his feet never touched the ground, and the streets passed fast until he was at our front door. I never doubted our son's story. Something similar happened to our daughter on my husband's watch.

It was the State Fair time in Oklahoma, the same month I had given birth to our son; our daughter was seven. My husband had told our daughter he would take her to the State Fair; remember, he was the fun parent. They went their merry way and had a wonderful time until my husband bent down to tie his shoe. When he got up from tying his shoe, our daughter was gone, and she was calling out for her dad, but he did not hear her. My husband, full of pride, would not yell our daughter's name; she could have been close to him.

Thinking creatively, our daughter thought she could call home, so she walked a block to the Shopping Mall to contact me. She told me that she had prayed before going to the mall. On her way to the Mall, she had no clue that it had closed for the night; she saw two ladies and a man who asked her what she was doing alone. She told the people she had lost her Dad, and she was going to call her mom. These kind people took her back to the State Fair; she told me the man placed her on his shoulders, thinking she might see her dad, but they saw a policeman first.

This was the first year the State Fair had a designated location for lost children. When my husband finally reached the area, there were wall-to-wall children, and our daughter was having fun! When our daughter saw her dad, she asked him what had taken so long to find her. Of course, she was not ready to leave, but she went along with her father. Her dad told me he had never been so scared in his life. Now he understood how I felt when losing our son!

Unlike our daughter, elementary school was a struggle for our son; to be honest, school was a struggle for him in general. His first experience with a Black teacher was among the worst teachers he encountered. It was a nightmare and discouraged our son from thriving in school. I had taught him never to be at the back of the class and to sit front and center so the teacher would know he was ready and willing to learn. However, because he was a taller student, the teachers regularly assigned him a seat in the back of the classroom. We all know from experience that most children sitting at the back of the room do not get the same attention as those up front.

Our home was less than thirty feet from the school, so we had a few times our son had to be a temporary latchkey child. It was an easy task for our daughter, and she had to walk much farther than thirty feet to make it home from elementary school. This was the beginning of my battle to prove that my son did not have Attention Deficit Disorder (ADD). Schools were receiving substantial amounts of funds for children with ADD, not my son! Also, when I had my son assessed for the disorder, the doctor who performed the testing had two daughters in elementary school labeled as ADD. Fortunately, neither her daughters nor my son had the disorder.

Thank the Lord, I read about Ben Carson and his brother's experience in public schools and how his mother fought for her sons. We know the end of the story: If you do not research his name and see what he accomplished in life! This caused a pattern with my son, from one grade to the next, of me having to make my presence known. It got to the point where I volunteered at the schools to ensure my son was getting what he needed and did not fall by the wayside. At one elementary school, it worked so well that the principal offered me a job as a teacher's aide. I was working on my associate degree, so there was no way I would give up my dream of obtaining a college degree. Our son graduated from elementary school and is now on to middle school!

Our son was in middle school, and unlike his sister, there were no bullies or intimidation because of his size; he was well-known for singing and was now making a name on the football field. I ensured my son continued in the fine arts by keeping choir in his curriculum until he graduated from high school and beyond. People knew he was a gentle giant unless you touched his lunch, and one classmate found out the hard way. Our son came home from school one day and told us he had to go to the principal's office for disruption in the cafeteria. One of his classmates had reached over onto his plate, taking a slice of pizza, and before our son realized what he had done, the boy went sliding across the room; this was the only encounter throughout his school years.

The older our son became, the more distant his dad became, and he spent less time with our family. Our daughter had graduated from high school and was in college. My son, husband, and I discussed how low our son needed to be when playing his defensive tackle position in football. Instead of his dad showing him the move, I was in our den illustrating the position and ran a play in the house; I pushed our son so hard that he bounced off the glass patio door, shattering it into pieces. The look on his face was sheer terror as he lost his balance and broke the glass door. I had no business showing our son how to play a position, and I had never played football.

Dad spent designated time attending our son's football games or talent shows at school. My husband carried over a high school habit called the dozens or ragging, often saying negative, demeaning things like," You bucket head Paul Bunion mountain shirt, husky jeans wearing pea brain." He used that sick humor as his so-called fun time with our son and often called him pea brain, comparing his brain to a dinosaur brain. I had a distaste for his style of humor, and it made me angry. I never joked with my children at all.

While listening to a talk show on the radio, I heard, "Mothers raise your son to be the type of man you want to marry." At the time, I thought that was brilliant and that his future wife would one day thank me. I was determined to mold my son into the man I wanted my husband to become. We would have mother and son dates to show him how a gentleman should treat a lady; make sure he opened the car and restaurant door, pull out her chair to assist her in adjusting her chair, ask what she preferred to eat, and then order for the table if it was not a buffet. It was successful for years until events changed my son's demeanor.

I tried my best to compensate for my husband's insensitive humor by using positive words to counteract the negative words spoken by his dad. I read that for every negative word spoken to a person, it takes ten positive words to cancel out the one negative word. I made the mistake of trying to fill shoes that were never designed for me to wear. This is where my son's coddling came into place.

His dad was all about joking, which was a mask not to reveal the hurt and pain that tormented his mind daily. My husband told me that it was my job to help the children learn. That aspect of my husband's attitude never changed. Not once did he ever help the children with their schoolwork. The responsibility fell onto my list of parental duties, even though my husband was better at math. I valued education more seriously than my husband.

In my first book, I discussed the differences my husband and I had, but I did not think education was an issue; it was massive. I discovered that even with education, my husband never spoke to the children about what they wanted to become when they grew up. I recall when our son was about ten. He said he wanted to do what his dad did for a living. I wanted to invest in our son's tutorial educational and extracurricular activities. My husband was all about the monetary impact, not positioning our children for academic success.

In my first book, I mentioned how this child was born out of manipulation; for years, I was saying he was born out of pure love; that was deception at its finest. My husband intentionally got me pregnant for a highly selfish reason discussed earlier. Years later, circumstances ushered that trait to manifest in our son. My son began to display similarities in his late twenties. The two started out being nothing alike; our son had a positive outlook on life. The negative traits were dormant, waiting for the perfect circumstance to activate generational spirits. As our son got older, he opened the door for them to flourish.

Neither our children nor I realized we were walking in deceit created by the lie my husband had lived for so many years. The whole family was walking in disappointment, as I thought my husband wanted our family. Time revealed he wanted the convenience of marriage without putting in the work for a good marriage. The language in our home was unresolved hurt; the primary factor was pain, and the results were anger.

Children are perfect illustrators; their actions tell you what happens in the family's household. Children will act out what Mom and Dad reveal at home, so be mindful of your actions, parents! The lack of mutual respect between a husband and wife will show up in the children, and then it is reaping time for what you, as a parent, have sowed.

Every child will mimic what they have absorbed; parents put all emotions in the atmosphere, so be mindful of what you say and do in your homes. The father is the parent responsible for watering the household with wisdom, knowledge, and understanding. He is to ensure positivity is flourishing among his family members. It is not the mother's responsibility, but that is what society has taught. The fathers are to set the atmosphere for the family. That responsibility has often been the responsibility of mothers here in America!

Children mimic what their parents show them; our children are no different. As I walked in deception, so did our children. Our daughter continued to be an outspoken, strong-willed individual. In contrast, our son continued to be the quiet, compliant, gentle giant who loved everybody, and the feelings were mutual everywhere he went. Both children were very impressionable, and their personalities were as different as day and night.

Both children's lives were more complicated than they should have been precisely because of my husband's and my poor communication skills in our marriage. But not in the aspect of having love, food, shelter, or clothing. I always ensured they had the best I could buy. I never bought brand-name clothes until later in life. I was the National Bank of Mom, there to provide whatever my children needed, predominantly for my son; my daughter was very independent and working by fourteen. Despite all that, my husband and I were living a dysfunctional marriage that produced dysfunctional children.

The constant arguments between my husband and me slowed down and were not as bad as when our children were eight and fifteen, but they were an everyday occurrence. Our children needed and deserved a God-led covenant home, with parents following God's word according to the Bible. We should have been unified, supportive parents who were available to discuss anything at any time. Yes, I was always present, but sad to say, I was not always emotionally present. I was more present with my son than my daughter; it was the opposite with her dad.

Could my husband have been jealous of our son, which triggered negative actions against our son? I recall that for every friend our son had come over to play, my husband would make negative statements about every boy, never attempting to get to know them. This occurred up until our son was in junior high school. Once our son began to sing frequently, at the age of thirteen, his dad stopped talking about his friends.

Living in a home where the leadership was out of order contributed to an unbalanced, dysfunctional family. Instead of a daughter learning femininity from her mother and a son seeing his father as a provider, protector, and leader in prayer, it was the opposite. I was trying to permeate my home with positive words from sermons, spiritual shows, gospel music, and much prayer. Bless my daughter's soul; around the age of sixteen, I know she got tired of waking up to me slinging anointed oil over her head and praying over her. I stopped that foolishness after learning the proper way to fight spiritually - with the word of God!

It took me years to become aware of the spiritual imbalance in our home. I knew I had to find a stable church home for our children. It was challenging to find a fit for what my family needed spiritually. Riding around the neighborhood, I found a Spirit-filled church, predominantly Caucasian, which was my preference. From my perspective, heaven will be multi-cultural, so we practiced on earth what would be in heaven. Pastor RF was an unconventional guy in every way. He would preach up and down the church aisle and fill the genuine office of the prophet. He would tell people what they had prayed to God, where they were, what they had on, and the position of prayer, kneeling, standing, or lying on the floor.

I will never forget the one time my husband went to church with my son and me, and Pastor RF revealed my husband's life like a book. He told him about his childhood hurts and mistreatments from his father, middle brother, and much more. My husband accused me of telling his business to Pastor RF, but I never spoke one thing about my husband. I did not need to; the man had a true gift from God. He prophesied to my husband, daughter, son, and myself. I have the tape to this day. Everything Pastor RF told us has happened!

This was the second confirmation that my son had a calling from God to be a preacher and teacher, spreading the gospel of Christ's eternal salvation. At that church, my son discovered many spiritual gifts and callings from God. My children are heavily gifted; my daughter is more spiritually anointed than her brother. As the eldest child, she should be. One embraced their spiritual gifts quicker than the other. The first time I heard such a thing was when I was thirty-three. Two times at Pastor RF's church, prophets told my children what was to come. At one point, a speaker talked about the gifts of the Holy Spirit, and my son, at eight years old, asked how many he could have. The speaker looked at him for about a minute and then told him, "God said you could have all of them!"

The first prophetic word of my son's spiritual calling came at the age of three from Mother S, the mother of my childhood classmate. We now had daughters who were best friends. My children and I attended Bible school with Mother S every weekend, and she always had a homemade snack. God does everything well; he used two generations to ensure his word about my son was spoken. God set all of that up for what was to come.

Mother S was an ancient wise woman of God. She gave my children a Bible Storybook, which had to be sixty years old. She was adamant about reading stories to my children, which I did regularly. She did not indulge in television or the things of the world. She was an older woman who relied on God to get her daily blessings. She was highly impactful not just in my children's lives but also in others! It was divine intervention that Mother S was the first person to see Christ in my son, daughter, and myself. She nurtured the gifts in us and made me aware of the precious gifts God had entrusted to me. We attended the bible study lessons with Mother S until we moved to Texas. She was indeed a blessing from the Lord above!

Once we moved to Plano, Texas, well-known companies hired me, especially after I acquired my associate's degree in Microcomputer Applications. That was the one field where I needed a strong personality, as I worked in a male-dominated field, and I could withstand anything they brought. I worked unusual shifts to accommodate our children, 3 pm to 11 pm,12 am to 8 am, and 11 pm to 7 am, which paid off financially. My husband was so comfort- able that he told his coworker (whose wife stayed home with their children), "Man, I have a working wife; I do not need to get a second job." That was my husband, who always had the goose that laid the golden eggs, and I took that role running with it for many years in the marriage. Money flowed freely, and I continued providing everything the children needed: clothes, shoes, and money for extracurricular activities. I was blessed to be able to provide for them.

Our son began to make his path in playing sports at six, recruited by a guy who could not believe he was only six, and paid everything needed to get our son on his baseball team. He began singing at eight years old, debuting in his elementary school talent show, singing Tevin Campbell's hit song "Can We Talk," while our daughter excelled academically. She never tried out for a swim team during high school, and I often wonder if that was due to her first experience in Richardson, Texas.

Unlike me, who wanted to run track but had to work at the dry cleaners, our daughter made the track team in high school but could not handle walking home after practice. There was one time after track practice when she called her dad to come pick her up. She was tired, and he should have done just that. The school was only four blocks from our home, so he told her to walk home. That was the first and last track practice our daughter attended. She put her focus on her high school sweetheart and going to college. Thank goodness, unlike me, her relationship did not end in marriage.

Now, our daughter was sixteen and smitten by the so-called perfect guy. I would come home from work, and my daughter would be gone. When I asked my husband where she was, he would tell me she had gone somewhere with her boyfriend, but he had no clue where they had gone. He was content if he had a stellar yard and received compliments from the neighbors on how well-groomed he kept his yard. His ego fed off positive affirmations of deeds.

My daughter followed her boyfriend's and dad's advice, and our son listened to his mom's advice. Our son was getting his feet wet in a puppy-love relationship. He reserved his heart for a little girl he had known from private school, which would be disastrous in later years—the years passed quickly!

Their Father's Cry For Help

ALL THE YEARS of negativity inflicted on our son were generated by their father's childhood issues. I did not understand that he was, and still is, crying out for help, but he was too prideful to accept the help that was offered. My husband used jokes to express thoughts about our son, putting negative words in the atmosphere that contributed to tearing down his self-esteem instead of building it up. Our son wanted his dad's favorable attention without having to sing or perform on the keyboard, play drums, or play football. He wanted unconditional love displayed by his dad, but his dad could not give what he had never had.

After putting the puzzle pieces together, now, it makes sense. My husband was remarkably close to his mother. At sixteen, he protected his mother, ensuring he was there when his dad came home. When my husband and I were dating, he would leave at a specific time because his mother was alone, but his reason was very dark. My husband shared with me that he saw his dad hit his mother in the mouth and knocked out her teeth when she said a cussword. That had to be devastating and scary to see such horrible treatment imposed upon his mother. He never mentioned any other physical abuse, but what man, the first time fighting his wife, knocks out her teeth? There had to be other occurrences of physical violence in his parents' marriage. This explains why my husband always told me, arguing, "At least you have all your teeth!"

I could never imagine my Dad raising a hand to my mother and never physically abusing her. Do not get me wrong, they had disagreements, but my wise mother knew how to keep my father in check without emasculating him. I was curious back then as to why he had to go, but now I get it; the way I protected our son was the same as my husband protecting his mother. However, my husband was never violent with our children when they were younger. That changed when they became young adults.

My husband lost his biggest supporter, his mother, to a bursting heart; nobody filled her place, but I became the substitute. My children suffered from their dad's unresolved childhood abandonment issues. I will not blame my husband for the circumstances that occurred when he was born into this world. However, once he became an adult, there were multiple opportunities to become aware of the driving forces in his life that caused him to display negative self-esteem issues and how they could have been restructured to create positive results.

The relationship between my son and his father gained momentum once our son turned twenty. Our son married at the age of twenty-six. Our son even purchased a motorcycle, believing it would bond their relationship in a positive light. There was little or often no male bonding, father-son time, no communication about life issues, and a shallow explanation of how the male anatomy functioned. No advice on how to treat a young lady, what to look for in a wife, how to prepare for a family, or how to resolve family issues. But once again, no deposit, no return!

I overstepped boundaries as the mother, addressing my husband's lack of actions in raising our son for many years. I should have allowed my husband to resolve issues with our son instead of constantly intervening. Did my husband even know how to fix problems? We never could as a couple! I should have removed myself. Instead, I felt the need to fill the gap in those areas to pass on to our son. The only time they spent regularly was watching football. Our son enjoyed watching the Dallas Cowboys. His dad did not have a favorite football team but often rooted for the underdog football team.

Despite my husband's flaws, our children appreciated having both parents in our home. At that time, divorce was at an all-time high. Three out of five was the ratio of our children's friends in broken homes due to divorce. Our daughter would often state how thankful she was to have a mother and father in the house.

She was the mature child conditioned from age four, hearing her parents argue, so it was just another day of dysfunctional normalcy. When our daughter married, the man was good, just like her dad was with me, but they both had deep, dark secrets as time revealed!

She Married A Man Like Dad

THE YEARS PASSED quickly. Our daughter scored high on her American Test (ACT), graduated from high school, and focused on college. Due to the many bright students in her graduating class of over one thousand, there were few scholarships within the school system.

She dreamed of going to college and getting a teaching degree, and I would do all I could to make that dream happen. I was working and making what I considered an excellent salary available for her to apply to attend college; I got a loan to cover her first year because I did not want to deplete my savings, which I needed much later. Please take note that I got the loan! She went to the same college as her boyfriend of four years, where he continued his cheating behavior, and their relationship ended quickly.

During our daughter's first year in college, my job terminated me for doing the right thing in a sexual discrimination case, so our daughter's dream of completing college fell short. There was no meeting of the minds with my husband to ensure our daughter could stay in college, but once again, I was on the island alone. At that time, my daughter did not have any information about how to file for grants, and had we known, she could have applied for a Pell Grant and continued her dream of gaining a college education.

She wanted to join the Marines; she could have been the first GI Jane long before the movie was released. Due to her intellectual ability, the marine recruiter convinced her to enlist in the Air Force. I always had our daughter covered in prayers, along with additional prayers from the women of my church. The favor of God shined upon my daughter, keeping her safe from the enemies' traps.

Our daughter's gift for teaching was utilized in the Air Force. Her military position was to train the pilots on an assimilating machine, gaining experience that could have led to an air traffic controller profession. Once our daughter explained the enormous stress attached to an air traffic controller position, we backed off trying to convince her to work in that field as a civilian at a major airline.

Years later, when my daughter was going to college again to complete her education, she joined an online church in Atlanta discovered by her brother while he was searching for spiritual truth; there had to be more than what we had experienced, and indeed, there was more. My son, daughter, and I were hungry for more of God. Eventually, she visited Atlanta and met a kind, handsome young man who was a church member. It did not take long for this young man to become smitten by our daughter and ask for her hand in marriage.

The only issue was that our daughter was attending college again in her thirties, on a scholarship, and working full-time, just like me in my thirties. Once again, her educational plans were disrupted, but she welcomed it this time. The wedding was a modest ceremony in the small church they attended. I made wedding reception arrangements and all decisions about the dinner menu by email since I was in Texas and the wedding was in Atlanta. The reception was excellent for the time allotted for planning. Nevertheless, the wedding was full of laughter and joy.

Our new son-in-law was more like a son than an in-law. He was very polite and sweet, and I could see why my daughter fell in love with him. We had a joke that my birth son was a baby boy, so we named my son-in-law baby boy number two! We immediately grew fond of him, even if he was a little on the quiet side. My birth son and our new son-in-law were good listeners. They both had keen ears to listen carefully, gather all information, and then speak logically and with a balance of reasoning; that is one characteristic I thought highly of in my son-in-law. But everyone has a dark side that will stay suppressed or will prevail.

Like me, my daughter thought she was getting a man who would love her until the end of her life. On the contrary, we married men with similar weak traits and lacked leadership in their families. The son-in-law was a younger, well-dressed, goal-oriented, and more educated version of her father. Her dad dressed nicely for work, thanks to me occasionally buying his clothes, but he needed to be more goal-oriented, and his only vision was to work and pay his bills. My daughter's husband was meticulous about his attire, looking like a GQ model.

My daughter's husband, a fraternal twin, was the least dominant of the two brothers, following the more decisive lead of his older twin brother. My mother had identical twin brothers; one was highly successful, and the other was always down and out! The bond of twin brothers was unknown to our daughter and immediate family. We did not realize that soul ties among twins are something that a spouse cannot comprehend. It can be a beneficial or detrimental experience.

Our sons-in-law's family embraced our daughter into theirs. His mother adored our daughter, just as my mother-in-law loved me long before I married her son. A few adjustment months were spent learning the personalities of her in-laws and how to deal with each of them positively in her new family.

Faithfully, our daughter was married and vowed she would not be the type of wife I was with her dad. I commend her for that, and I am sure her husband appreciated that decision. Our daughter would not be combative but communicate as mature adults should in a marriage. Her husband was an excellent communicator, so they did very well in that area of their marriage. Where their marriage fell short was the shift her husband needed to make from a single man to understanding he was now a husband and how important it was to spend quality time by solidifying his relationship with his wife.

Like me, my daughter loves to travel. One of their favorites was Hilton Head in South Carolina. I had scheduled annual family cruises, so they were up for the 7-day cruises. Our first family cruise had its bumps, but nothing involving my daughter and her husband. They knew how to stay clear of the line of fire when things were not going so well with my marriage or other family disputes.

Our son-in-law's parents were never married; he came from a single-parent home and did not experience the highs and lows of married parents growing up. Our son-in-law was shocked when my husband and I had a yelling match. We were conditioned to argue in front of anybody and had no filters. Our daughter's husband would not get involved, but he did not like the arguing.

On my son-in-law's first visit to Texas, friction between my husband and I was so bad that our son-in-law was ready to catch a plane and return to Atlanta. He was traumatized. Our daughter had to explain to him that this is what she grew up with daily. I acted a plum fool before my son-in-law; at that time, there was not one sign of femininity in me. I now embrace and appreciate my feminine qualities; as a lady, I have embraced my femininity and love every aspect of being a woman. The only masculinity I want to see is in a man!

Three years passed, and our daughter's marriage was less cohesive than she would have liked. However, they continued to attend our family trips. We cruised to Jamaica, Grand Cayman, Cancun, Cozumel, Playa del Carmen Puerta Villarta, and other islands. Our favorite annual trip was to Las Vegas, and it was always fun. My daughter also went on her husband's family trips to Ohio.

During our final cruise, baby boy number two was distant from our family due to our family dysfunction. He did not talk as much as he usually would have. He kept to himself, watching March Madness on the television instead of enjoying himself, as on previous cruises and family trips. Typically, he would make jokes and smile, but he was very distant on our final cruise. I labeled this our final cruise because we have never been on any more cruises since this one. That was the end of an era.

Little did our daughter know that her husband, like her dad, kept secrets from his wife. Like her dad, our son-in-law was living a lie of a marriage. Also, just like her dad, her husband was not there to defend and protect his wife when attacked by Pastor S, in the absence of her husband's presence, who often said things to our daughter about her family after we left his congregation.

Our ambitious son-in-law wanted to return to school for his master's degree, which would have opened more excellent career advancement opportunities. After talking with our daughter about his goal, he pursued it. Like my husband, our son-in-law was stellar at saving money, and why wouldn't he be? His master's was in Finance. Once he completed his graduate degree, opportunities flourished.

Out of nowhere, our daughter called to tell us that my son-in-law wasn't feeling the same about their marriage as she did. Initially, he made it seem like his feelings weren't as strong as those of my daughters. We called him and explained that marriage has its ups and downs. We encouraged him to stay the course and were sure his doubts would pass. After a year, he said he was no longer in love with our daughter. He executed his plan discreetly and quietly and eventually left our daughter. Unlike her mother, she worked so hard to be a good wife. Unknowingly, our son-in-law had been planning for a few years to divorce our daughter, and when he initiated his plan, she was devastated.

She kept living in the townhouse they had moved to, and he went his merry way, starting over. We had jokingly told our son-in-law, just as my mother told my husband, "If you don't want her, bring her back to us." Our son-in-law gave that no thought, just as my husband gave that saying no thought. Our son-in-law never called us to let us know anything when he divorced our daughter, which included us as well.

The divorce between our daughter and now ex-son-in-law was very civil and drama-free. Even though it was unexpected for our daughter, she handled it gracefully, although deep down, I was unaware that she was holding bitterness within. Months after our daughter divorced, I wanted to ensure she was doing okay, so I visited her for two weeks. This gave us time to bond.

She had a great support system while she was going through her divorce; her ex-sister-in-law (who was married to his twin and now divorced) kept her included in family functions and gatherings. She also had surrogate parents and bible study teachers who would have her over once a week for bible study and dinner. Thank God my daughter was not alone during the pre-divorce and post-divorce process.

We wanted our daughter to return to Texas after her divorce so we could be there for emotional support. However, she decided to remain in Atlanta until returning to Texas in 2022, unaware that she was returning to support her mother spiritually. I am so grateful she listened to God's voice and returned home at the perfect time!

He Married the Opposite of Mom

OUR SON WAS twelve when he started attracting young girls. He was his dad's height, and they wore size twelve wide shoes. We purchased shoes every birthday as our son's feet grew. At age 16, his feet stopped growing. It was costly to buy a size 16 pair of shoes back then, but the National Bank of Mom was there to supply the funds for the expenses.

I thought it was good for our son and daughter to get some work experience. When our son was thirteen, I signed him up to work as a swimming instructor at a local recreation center. His sister taught him to swim; he was also like a fish in the water, so that was his first job. Our daughter had a flair for name-brand clothes, so I altered her birth certificate to make her a year older so she could work at a department store.

Our son was a natural salesperson. At the age of ten, he received a catalog to sell items, and once he reached a specific amount, he could select a gift. He selected a telescope as his goal, which motivated him to sell enough items to order the telescope. He never met a stranger; selling was easy for him. That is one favorable trait that his dad had, especially at work, where the best of himself was reserved for his jobs.

Middle school brought more exposure to football, as did his singing regularly at school and talent show competitions, and girls gravitated to it. He also caught the eyes of the church girls. We found a church in Plano, TX, and attended it for thirteen years. Many mothers wanted to match their daughters with our son because he was a young man who loved God.

I had to tactfully confront two young girls who decided to visit our son at our home unannounced. One of their fathers drove the girls over and waited in his car for them to visit our son. The father never got out of the car to introduce himself or check out the environment inside our home. We could have been weird people. I explained to the young girls that it was not appropriate for girls to visit a boy, especially unannounced; that was to be the other way around. Of course, diverse cultures have different views on that subject. Our son never had other girls come to our house to see him.

One young lady became very close to our son and our family. Her parents were ambitious and fell in love with our son, as many mothers and fathers had. Both were in the choir and became regular escorts for each other during dances and events. They made an attractive couple, but it never progressed beyond a loyal, close friendship. Her family was not originally from America but from the motherland. I enjoyed their family events, and we were always invited to attend their gatherings. To this day, our son keeps in touch with this young lady, who is now a Physician.

His first love was also a manipulator who was in it for the fame and fortune she thought was coming to our son. My son fell in love with this girl when they attended a private school. She was his father's pick, not mine. I had selected one of our pastor's daughters who would have been a better fit for our son. She was beautiful, with long hair, and had that wholesome, girl-next-door look with a smile that lit up any room. Her parents were fun to hang out with occasionally.

Our son's first love resembled Beyoncé in terms of face and body. Her parents were motorcycle lovers, and we enjoyed their company and occasionally went on motorcycle rides together. The same pattern of four years of a lie of a relationship occurred with this young lady. She strung our son along and caused heartache during their time of what I considered courting. She kept his mind in a fog of confusion that affected his high school and college studies. Like his dad, his relationship lasted four years also but did not lead to marriage. After the breakup with his Beyoncé look-alike, our son met someone he thought was his forever person.

Our son's second love was more like me than his first love. Unlike the first immature girlfriend, this young lady was level-headed, mature, and knowledgeable about spiritual things. Although she had been raised without her father in the house, she did have the opportunity to stay with her father, stepmother, and half-sister on occasions in Plano, TX. They met on one of her visits with her dad; she had come to church just at the right time.

She enlightened our son about the dangers of specific genres of music and introduced him to GCL, an expert in that arena. She and her mother had no easy lifestyle. She knew how to survive. I could see this young lady as a permanent family member, and I welcomed her with open arms. Our son fell hard for this young lady and bought her an engagement ring months later. She was in college and had gone to a fraternity party. When our son found out, he tried to chastise her actions, but she put him in his place and broke off their relationship. No man would tell her where she could not go if she chose to do so.

When they broke up, the absolute love of his life almost caused him to have a nervous breakdown. His sister helped him buy an engagement ring, and he traveled to Houston to get her back. He did not know where she lived, nor did he have her new phone number, but he located where she lived and confronted her about the breakup. With characteristics like his mom, she was strong-willed and refused to be controlled by any man who told her what she could and could not wear or where to go. Unlike his mom, when they broke up, there was no reconciliation or giving a chance after chance, as I did with his dad. She is now married and an educator.

After the devastating breakup, our son placed an invisible wall up so he would not get hurt again. At the same time, he longed for a companion to spend the rest of his life with. Our son was twenty-six and longing to have a mate for life. At fourteen, he had taken a class at church, where he vowed to save himself for marriage before becoming intimate with a woman. Each student who attended the class received a purity ring promising to wait for marriage before having sexual intimacy. He kept his promise to God.

The years of waiting for his forever person did not come without more sorrow and heartache, but the day finally came when he met his forever person. It was nothing but fate that these two joined in wedlock. Once again, our son gravitated to a young lady whose parents never married. She was raised by her innovative, intelligent, and wise mother. They met on BlackPeopleMeet.com, which cost a fee to participate. I have often heard our son tell people that it was his best investment to pay his last fifteen dollars to extend his membership instead of buying a box of Golden Chicken that would have cost precisely fifteen dollars.

I commend my daughter-in-law's mother for sheltering her two daughters from corruption in Dayton, Ohio. Seeing a responsible, mature, innocent young lady like her was refreshing. Our new daughter's father lived in Texas, and he, too, is a very intellectual man. We had a new family member in less than a year, and our son was the happiest we had ever seen him. When we were all together at a Mall, they were like two big children holding hands and skipping down the sidewalk. I prayed for a tall wife, and the prayer was answered, as she stands six feet tall, with legs as long as stilts.

Being sheltered from the world has pros and cons. I had to teach some things to my new daughter as I looked at her and treated her not as a daughter-in-law but as a daughter. I will not point out all the things, but some were common knowledge she lacked due to her sheltering. There were movies, TV shows, and songs that she needed to learn about. Even though I had no boundaries in my marriage, at the time of this new marriage, I had told myself I would stay within my limits and not invade their marriage. I would not be the nagging mother-in-law who made my new daughter cringe whenever I walked into their home. I had reserved the nagging for my now ex-husband. I am sure he would agree!

The drawback of being hurt by his two previous loves affected his relationship with his wife. Our son had to learn that he could not deprive his wife of honesty and affection because of past events. He could not allow the past hurts to dictate his future and have him shortchange the one who would bear his children. With much understanding and patience from his wife, her husband finally apologized for not expressing his emotions to her.

Three years have passed since the wedding union, and now our new daughter and son are involved in a radical organization with a hidden agenda. Our son had researched several groups, and this was a dominant group that often confronted people on the streets. This group separated people according to ethnicity and was proud and boastful, putting a wedge in immediate families and creating versions of families. Their beliefs were contrary to what the bible taught about the love of Jesus.

My husband and I were separated from our son and daughter for eight months. No phone calls or visits, only the ability to view them on social media, enjoying gatherings with strangers that were foreign to his parents! With constant, faithful, fervent prayer, ties were severed by the radical group. Leaders of the group needed to be loyal; they preached one thing but lived another. Our daughter consistently called and checked on her parents as she always did, and our son had gone away! When we finally reunited, our new daughter was four months pregnant.

My son knew I had been preparing to become a grandmother for over eighteen years. I had everything needed for arrival: books, clothes, shoes, baby carriers, and educational toys. I had been purchasing neutral items for years. My family would laugh at me whenever I came home with new baby items. In my opinion, I was going to be the best grandmother ever! I had made a conscious effort to have boundaries and not to be a nagging mother-in-law. However, I did not consider applying those exact boundaries to become a grandmother.

Our daughter-in-law was nervous about carrying the baby, as her only sibling, a sister, could never have a child. She had several miscarriages, and now our daughter-in-law was terrified she would suffer the same results. Blessings were upon the pregnancy, but our first grandchild was born months earlier than anticipated, weighing 2 pounds and 2 ounces. All four grandparents were there when the hospital staff rolled out this tiny bundle of joy to the Neonatal Intensive Care Unit (NICU) that would impact my life. My life would never be the same! I had made my marriage an idol; now, life revolves around this little blessing!

At the time, our son was working as a correctional officer at the county jail, while his mother-in-law was a live-in nanny helping with the needs of our premature grandson. Like his father, the pressure of now having a child to be responsible for was more than our son anticipated. He was familiar with the needs of a baby, but it is different when it is your child and not one in a church nursery. It was a blessing to have a grandmother living in the home to assist with the adjustment of becoming a parent.

Four months later, it was time for our daughter-in-law's mother to leave and let the new parents implement their parenting skills. Maternity leave had ended, and it was back to the grind of both parents working. It worked out perfectly because I was no longer working, so I became the babysitter. I was eager to step up to the challenge, and it put some money in my pocket. Of course, I spent most of it buying clothes for our new grandson!

Our daughter-in-law has always favored organic, holistic eating habits, so that was the guideline for our grandson. There was no baby cereal at two months old like his dad, soft scrambled eggs, mashed potatoes, cornbread soaked in greens juice, and no sweets unless they were natural from fruits. I respected her rules as I, too, blended all my children's baby food from fresh vegetables so they would have natural food.

I had waited so many years for a grandchild, so naturally, I did not follow all my daughter-in-law's guidelines. I used code words when giving our grandson things his mother would not. Grandmother had taught the baby how to lie; he would call non-GMO tortilla chips, apples, and homemade cookie crackers, but eventually, I got exposed when he learned how to say cookie from his grandfather. Breaking the feeding rules caused friction between my daughter-in-law and me, but we lived in two different cities, so I agreed not to break her rules, only to do the opposite when my grandson was in my home.

Our son often expressed that he would not marry a woman who was not submissive and honored him as the head of his household. He also married someone who fit the criteria. Like his sister, he stayed true to what he had professed for many years. Out of my dysfunctional marriage, both children knew what they did not want in a spouse.

Our daughter-in-law used her biblical teachings and followed them regarding what type of wife she has proven to be: one who allows her husband to lead the family, even if it might not be the best decision for the family at that given time. I commend her for having that characteristic. She constantly sought ways to honor her husband and let him know she always had his back.

Years of observing how our daughter-in-law has dealt with our son proves that prayer changes how a husband listens. Soft words turn away wrath, and it is easier to accomplish things. In essence, she is a submissive wife in the fashion that works best for her husband. There were times she submitted so he would be happy, and she expressed that to me early in their marriage.

Our son did not marry a woman like his mom. Yes, his wife has a spicy, sassy side, but she knows when to let it shine and when to keep it under wraps. She also knows how to communicate and keep the conversation civil. Most importantly, she is the submissive wife that I tried to be many times in my marriage, but it never solidified. However, we have similar qualities—drive, ambition, and determination to achieve goals.

Surviving The Aftermath

FORTY-THREE YEARS into the marriage, we made a massive change in our lifestyle. Unexpected circumstances carved our future, or was God directing my family to the truth necessary for a new direction in life? In 2016, my husband finally retired after his near-death experience, as discussed in my first book. I prayed for God to spare my husband's life. I was not ready to become a widow. God answered my prayer, having mercy on my husband after four surgeries in seven days.

I was so wrapped up in being a grandparent that we made a crucial, irreversible mistake. I convinced my husband to sell our home in the city where our children grew up and finally move onto our son's land now that we have a grandson. I wanted to be as close as possible, and thirty feet away is as close as almost living with them. We lived with our son's family for two weeks until our differences caused us to get put out, and we had to sleep in our newly manufactured home with no electricity in the heart of winter. This was another sign of what will happen in the future.

My husband and I had to spend money to clear the land before moving to our son's property. We had to pay for six giant trees to get cut down to make room for our double-wide manufactured home. Whatever needed to be done was worth the cost to be close to that precious grandchild. I had offered to purchase an acre of our son's land, but our son would not sell us the acre of land. We also covered the driveway with asphalt and created a driveway for our vehicles beside the main driveway. Living thirty feet from our grandchild was expensive, but he was worth every dollar spent.

Grandparents sometimes have greater insight into what might work as parents; this is the opportunity to get the things right that should have been implemented when raising their children. There are areas of child-rearing that young parents do not give a second thought to. Instead of appreciating our wisdom, our son and daughter-in-law discarded our ideas and would often get offended.

History repeats itself for sure. I made my grandson an idol, putting this little bundle of joy as my filler from a sinking marriage and breakdown of communication. The sun and moon revolved around this grandchild, so much so that, one time, I told his parents I was my grandson's surrogate parent. I poured myself into my grandson; little did I know this created a similar pattern of defending and protecting my grandson, just as I had done with my son and his father. Once again, I had gone off the deep end, just as I had done with my marriage.

My personality had not transformed to where I am now, so my actions always benefited my grandson and fulfilled the joy of spending time with him. The obsession was so intense that it made my husband jealous to see me enjoying my grandson's company so much. In my opinion, my husband was excessively rough with our grandson, to the point of him telling me his grandfather was mean. That child saw what it took me years to see with clear eyes.

Four years later, along came another grandson. While the first grandson was all about his grandmother, this child was all about his grandfather. Rightfully so, the new grandson looked like his grandfather's mini-me for several years. So now, as grandparents, we both had much joy brought to us by these boys. The excessive roughness did not let up with the second grandson, but he was tough. Crying for him was not an option. He would come back swinging, giving his grandfather a good challenge.

Just as a tsunami has an aftermath, so has the actions of my dysfunctional marriage, which caused there to be with everyone involved. Just like the aftermath of a devastating event, some people recover faster, while other people relive the traumatic experience continuously in their minds. Half of the family faces the hurtful truth, committed to change for the better. Meanwhile, the other half of the family walks in degrees of deception, praying the truth will eventually enlighten them. We all survived some difficult times that have left permanent scars. Some family members take longer to heal, while others are eager to move forward in the light of truth. Some wounds are slowly scabbing over and will not completely heal until the truth is accepted instead of embracing a strong lie.

If anyone were ever a survivor, it would genuinely be the eldest child in my family. Our daughter survived the aftermath of the divorce, realizing the man she married was not her forever person. She has survived the aftermath of being falsely accused of being an instigator in my marriage dissolving. She survived the ridicule of a younger brother whose eyes are clouded and whose judgment is inaccurate. Now that the sorrow and heartache have passed, instead of getting upset, prayers are spoken for her brother's eyes to be opened and his heart renewed in Jesus and salvation for her father.

As my transformation continues to heal me, destiny calls, and I am answering. The aftermath made me more substantial through the exchange of Jesus's strength for my weakness, and where there was sadness, now joy resides.

For my son, we have not had any form of positive communication, but it is coming soon. Surviving the aftermath has him in a different frame of mind that I don't quite understand, but everyone has different coping methods. He has survived the aftermath, thinking he knows how my new life has unfolded, but his conclusions have no validity. This child always had his mother on his side until he became someone I did not recognize reasonably. I know that, with him, just as I have, he will find God's truth.

Surviving the aftermath has taught me how to adjust and adapt with consistent effort, which I could not have accomplished without divine guidance. I have faced ALL my errors as a mother, taking a long look at what I contributed to my dysfunctional marriage that bled emotions of turmoil all over my children. But becoming the best version God created me to be will only benefit my children and grandchildren in the future.

I will never allow old lies to invade my thoughts. I have learned from many years of mistakes and know it will be a continuous process to keep myself on the positive path of life. I will keep myself humble, value my destiny, and be aware of others' feelings.

Staying on course and accomplishing things I had only dreamed of doing is exciting, especially exploring in the latter years of my life. My life is flourishing at 71, and I have never felt more alive. With every stroke of each word written, I exude joy, looking forward to my future!

Broken Curses Of Bondage

CONQUERING THE POWER of manipulation will forever be a process. Still, with the guidance of the Holy Spirit and obedience to the instructions, I am meeting the challenge of putting in work and effort to keep it at bay in my life. How does ne do that? Stay in tune with God daily, listen to his guidance, read his word, and surround yourself with positive people who stand for the same things you stand for in life. Show yourself caring for those who may have done you wrong and on the verge of losing hope. I often do what my natural father frequently said, "If you do right by people, right will come to you.

Exposing Satan, the enemy or opposition, is key to conquering manipulation. Once a negative person, place, or thing has been called out in my life, it can no longer cause me to have secrets or be controlled by that issue. There were hidden secrets in the debts of my unconscious memory, only to be revealed by truth and healing, contributing to my transformation. When guilt, shame, and anger existed, they would rise to the surface, causing discomfort, irritation, and sometimes physical pain; that is how I know I am reaching the core of the secret places where the enemy has kept those things to keep me down. But no demon in hell can keep me from my God-given destiny if I am determined to live my kingdom life.

The opposition would discourage me, my immediate family, and my generations from moving forward in Christ. I WILL continue to follow how my Father in Heaven directs me, praying every day, believing there will be a brighter future for all my current and former family members, yes, even my ex-husband. I will continue to pray for his salvation, even if he never speaks to me again. I will pray that he receives healing for all the hurt he endured most of his life and pray that he finds the happiness he desires in life.

He is the father of my children, and even if my intimate love for him no longer exists, there should be some cordiality between us. We produced some of the most extraordinary, intellectual human beings worth celebrating. The words speak of only a good tree that can bear good fruit and a bad tree that bears bad fruit; I see good fruit falling from the tree, but good fruit will rot if it stays on the ground.

God's voice is more precise as he speaks through his Holy Spirit, residing inside of me! I will continue following the straight and narrow course no matter how illogical it may sound. My Father in Heaven is not a God of logic, and often, his instructions are the opposite of what our minds would tell us to do. If I should miss the mark, and sometimes I will, I ask God for forgiveness and do better the next day! I am experiencing that the more obedient I am, the greater the instruction comes from God, along with unexpected and expected blessings.

One miraculous blessing I saw in a vision was the mighty hand of God hitting the house of familiar spirits like a wrecking ball; the house tumbled down as each brick shattered into rubble from the house that had a supernatural grip on my family. These were the familiar spirits: pride, lying, fantasizing, blocked intimacy, self-righteousness, control, bitterness, sensuality, abandonment, rage, malice, judgment, criticism, neglect, and isolation. That house will never be rebuilt, and I will continue to do what is necessary to keep it dismantled. This was a significant sign that I was gaining spiritual confidence.

My walk with God has become more profound, and my prayer life is substantially stronger as I walk in dedimus power and authority, just as Jesus walked on this earth. Do you know why? Because he lives in me, I know the great exchange that was made for me to have eternal life with Christ. I will not tread over the Blood of Jesus to accept what the world offers. Life is filled with blessings, small and large. And I enjoy each day, even when it is not the best. Thank you, Father, for your gift of the Holy Spirit that dwells in me!

What awaits me in the future? A life of blessing others through my books, websites, Podcasts, and soon-to-be-established ministry. I will help other women who will become displaced and need a helping hand, just as I received when I was a displaced woman. I am a modern-day Lydia, constantly blessed to be a blessing to others. There are women and children whose lives I will impact. My destiny is calling me loud and clear, and I am on my way to answering right here, right now!

In Book 2, She Is My Daughter, He Is His Son, I have once again been transparent about how my dysfunctional marriage affected my children. I hope this book helps reveal some insight, spiritual nuggets, and inspiration. I firmly believe that everything happens for a reason, and this book would not exist without my circumstances. I am not done telling you my story, but this book is precious and dear to my heart because of my precious children, current in-laws, ex-laws, and grandchildren.

The future holds more stories to share with my readers. The next book will be "Life After 50 Years of Marriage," which will share the adjustment of becoming a single woman for the first time, including all the twists and turns of events that have transpired since 2022. I cannot wait to share all the positive things to come. As an old song said, "The best is yet to come.